BODY NEUTRALITY

The Liberating Practice of Accepting
Your Body Exactly as It Is

Ayla Freitas Ghibaudy

Copyright © 2021 Ayla Freitas Ghibaudy

All rights reserved. This book or any portion thereof may not be reproduced or used in any manner whatsoever without the express written permission of the publisher except for the use of brief quotations in a book review.

This book is not intended as a substitution for medical advice. The reader should consult a physician in matters relating to their health and particularly with respect to any symptoms that may require diagnosis or medical attention. The reader should not make any changes to their diet or regular health plan without consulting a physician.

Edited by Kaity Konsulis. Proofread by Nico Ghibaudy. Cover Art by Anna Douglas.

ISBN: 979-8-5807-5831-2

For my mom, who always tells me I have something to say.
For my dad, who makes me feel like I can do anything.
For my husband, who reminds me of my worth every day.

"i reduced my body to aesthetics
forgot the work it did to keep me alive
with every beat and breath
declared it a grand failure for not looking like theirs
searched everywhere for a miracle
foolish enough to not realize
i was already living in one"

                    RUPI KAUR, THE SUN AND HER FLOWERS

CONTENTS

Title Page	2
Copyright	3
Introduction	12
Negative Body Image	15
Diet Culture	25
Body Positivity: A Flawed Solution	42
The Practice of Body Neutrality	47
Strategy 1: Self-Talk	54
Strategy 2: Neutral Language	62
Strategy 3: Self-Care	69
Conclusion	76

INTRODUCTION

◆ ◆ ◆

A few years ago I decided it was a good idea to quit my well-paying, stable day job to pursue a new career. Filled with altruism and boredom, I was no longer satisfied working in business and wanted to start working in health and wellness in some capacity. As a notorious non-risk-taker, I surprised myself by actually going through with it. I enrolled in the Nutritional Therapy Practitioner (NTP) program with the Nutritional Therapy Association in 2019.

When I graduated, I was ready to change the world. As a fresh, doe-eyed NTP, I was eager to get out there and share all I had learned about the human body and holistic nutrition. But then I hit a bump in the road.

When I looked to the leaders in the nutrition profession, I was discouraged to find many of them peddling fad diets and focusing on weight loss. I felt a dissonance—they preached health and wellness but their words didn't match their programs or services.

This sent me into a tailspin. Is this whole profession a farce? Does anyone legitimately care about nutrition science? Or is it all just vanity?

That's when I discovered the Anti-Diet movement. Finding

this movement of practitioners (NTPs, RDs, MDs, etc.) who shared my convictions felt like coming home. I connected deeply to the words of incredibly intelligent professionals who understand that nutrition is just a *piece* of the health puzzle (albeit an important piece) because health is very complicated. They understand that nutrition therapy is needed in the right context—context that has no room for diet culture.

This wave of dietitians and physicians who are willing to break through social norms to advocate for their patients gives me hope. Although this movement is small and has yet to break into mainstream, conventional medicine, it is mighty.

More than half of all women struggle with negative body image. Diet culture has caused serious damage, but there is hope. There are a growing number of health providers creating a safe environment for people of all sizes, and that is a beautiful thing.

This Anti-Diet movement helped me make peace with food, and it also led me to the body neutrality movement, which helped me make peace with my body. Body neutrality gave me the clarity I needed to recognize that the problem is not my body or the way I feel about it. The problem is our culture.

If you are looking for a different, more healthy way to view your body, I wrote this for you. The practice I outline in this book is a way to reconcile your relationship with your body no matter how complicated it is—a way to come into yourself.

I'm not going to try to convince you of anything. My intent is simply to present you with a different perspective. The work of changing a deeply-ingrained belief is vigorous, intimate work that you can't be coaxed into.

I hope these pages leave you feeling encouraged and bolstered. I hope you feel inspired to live a life unhindered by body hate. I hope you find body neutrality as wildly liberating as I do.

NEGATIVE BODY IMAGE

◆ ◆ ◆

I have this collection of memories in my mind that I have unconsciously held onto since I was a young girl. These memories have stood the test of time when countless others have blurred and grayed. Growing up, my mom would take me with her to her manicurist's house. I can still vividly see the small back-bedroom-turned-home-salon. It was a constant bustle of movement as clients came and went, lap dogs meandered, and hungry children came to inquire about lunch. Fast-talking Brazilian women dished gossip with enthusiasm. I would sit quietly and observe, speaking only when directly asked a question. The tias I encountered here didn't pay me much mind besides to say one thing, usually to my mom —"She is *so* pretty".

Was it true? I had heard that complement from other family members, mostly aunts and grandparents gushing at a holiday dress or my long, wild curls. But coming from a stranger, somehow this compliment seemed stronger and truer. This stranger did not love me, so surely they'd have no reason to make such a statement were it not true. But perhaps that's just what people said about other people's kids. Yet, I held onto those words each time I heard them. I held onto them because I knew *pretty* was a good thing to be, and I wanted to be all the good things—studious, popular, creative, smart, kind, and so on.

As a kid, I didn't think too much about the way I looked, at least until someone else mentioned something about it. So how I felt about my physical appearance was almost completely determined by the people around me. The messages were mixed—not everyone agreed with the salon tias. I'll never forget the time my school friend Brandon came up behind me and shook my arm. "Why are your arms so jiggly" he jeered at my 11 year-old self. That was around the age I noticed I didn't look like most of my friends. They were long and lean where I was soft and a little rounder. When we sat side by side in a minivan, my thighs smushed down to twice the size of theirs.

I remember looking at magazine spreads of beautiful, svelte supermodels and feeling this unfamiliar pang in my gut. Envy. I didn't know what to call it then, but envy and I became well acquainted over the years. My family members loved to say I looked like Cindy Crawford as a way to affirm the moles—excuse me, "beauty marks"—on my face. But my thighs and belly sure didn't look like Cindy Crawford's. And it surely didn't help that puberty forget to transform me into a shapely, feminine goddess.

As my interest in boys grew, so did my insecurity about my body. As a teenager, I liked to think I was down-to-earth and low maintenance because I wasn't interested in makeup or flat irons. I don't think I was unencumbered by societal pressure as much as I was unwilling to appear as though I were "trying" to be beautiful, lest I fail miserably. But I desperately wanted to be beautiful. I walked through school halls analyzing each pair of eyes I met. "What do they think of me?" "Does he find me attractive?" It was incredibly distracting and frequently demoralizing.

These were the formative experiences that shaped my relationship with my body. I think most women can pinpoint moments like these. The first words spoken about your appearance. The first thoughts and feelings about a particular body part. The growing sense that *pretty* is a very important trait to have and keep. We all had different childhoods, but we can probably all relate to this: somewhere along the road, the relationship turned sour. Our bodies become a thing to be judged and compared, to be obsessed with or hated. But that's not all a body is for, and I wish I had known that as a girl. I wish I had known a body is meant for so much more than looking at.

Before we get into negative body image, let's take a moment to consider what body image even is. Close your eyes and imagine your physical appearance. What do you see? Take a moment and really envision yourself. What features stick out to you the most? How do you feel about those features? For me, I see a tall, tan woman with a wild head of brown hair and a face decorated with moles. Most days, this image doesn't make me feel much of anything. Afterall, It's just me! On a bad day, though, this image might bring up feelings of frustration, envy, or disappointment.

Your own personal body image is made up of how you see your physical self plus the thoughts and feelings that accompany that image. This is a simple concept, but it has profound implications.

The way you see yourself is influenced by both internal factors and environmental factors. Your inner thoughts and feelings impact your body image, but so does the world around you. Body image is thought to have four aspects: perceptual, affective, cognitive, and behavioral.

- *Perceptual body image* is how you see yourself.

- *Affective body image* is how you feel about your appearance.

- *Cognitive body image* is what you think and believe about your body.

- *Behavioral body image* is the behavior you engage in as a result of your body image.

Studies show that over half of Americans are dissatisfied with their bodies and it's even lower if you only count the women. Negative body image is widespread. It's common for people to have negative internal and environmental factors affecting their body image. It's common for people to have negative perceptions, feelings, thoughts, and behaviors regarding their bodies. It's common to see yourself in a mirror and not like the image that stares back.

But like I always say regarding any symptom or health issue: just because it's *common*, doesn't mean it's *normal*. If you're reading this, odds are you know exactly what I'm talking about. You know what it's like to have a negative body image because you've lived it. Before I even go into the consequences of negative body image, you already know what they are because you've experienced them. But please know, you don't have to settle. You don't have to accept your reality as "normal" or "fine" or "something you just need to get over." You don't have to hate your body.

Self Image

Your body image is only a *part* of your self image; your body is a single slice of the whole pie that makes you who you are. Your self image is how you see and feel about your entire self. There are many different schools of thought regarding the different aspects of self image. Some say that self image can be summed up in three parts:

- How we see ourselves physically—I have brown hair, brown eyes, and am pretty tall.

- Our social roles—I am a daughter, wife, friend, writer, marketing coordinator, and church member.

- Our personality traits—I am loyal, doubtful, and sociable.

Some would contend there are more than just those three categories. Suzaan Oltmann, an independent distributor at one of South Africa's FET Colleges, proposed that there are actually six dimensions:

- Physical dimension: how you evaluate your appearance.

- Psychological dimension: how you evaluate your personality.

- Intellectual dimension: how you evaluate your intelligence.

- Skills dimension: how you evaluate your social and technical skills.

- Moral dimension: how you evaluate your values and principles.

- Sexual dimension: how you feel you fit into society's masculine/feminine norms (Oltmann, 2014).

Self image is important because it directly impacts self-esteem, or how you value yourself. In other words, self-image determines what you think you're worth. Cultivating a healthy self-image is not a vain or trivial pursuit. If you don't believe you have value or worth, that is going to seep into every aspect of your life and everything you do—and it's going to cause harm.

Body image is only one part of overall self image. This makes sense because you are more than just a body. You're a complex creature with a body and skills and morals and thoughts and a personality and social roles. So why do we focus so much on body image? Why does it have the power to destroy our self-image and consequently, our self worth? It's because society has placed beauty on a pedestal. We have made outward appearances far more important than they should be.

Historical Body Ideals

Society places an absurd amount of emphasis on outward appearances, especially for women. Women are expected to be beautiful. But the thing is, society makes beauty an elusive, ever-changing bullseye. Throughout history, the ideal shape for women has changed tremendously. In ancient Greece, it was the full, round Aphrodite-esque body. In the 1950s the end of the Great Depression gave way to the hourglass figure. Then in the 1960s it was all about the long and slender youthful look. You get the idea.

In each era, through each beauty standard, one thing was constant: beauty standards caused harm to the women who tried to uphold them. Women have endured a lot through the ages, just to be deemed beautiful.

Foot Binding, the practice of wrapping the feet of young girls to modify their shape and size, was commonplace in China for a thousand years. The price of tiny feet was pain and sometimes infection or sickness. In the Victorian era, corsets were considered an essential part of feminine fashion. Their tight laces could shrink a waist down to as small as 17 inches around, all the while rearranging organs and restricting breathing.

The idea of an "ideal" shape reduces women to objects. It

makes it so that women can be graded on a pass-fail basis. It distorts a woman's view of herself because she is no longer free to be who she was made to be; she now has to fit some standard to be valuable.

I feel compelled to note, I am not implying men cannot have a distorted body image—society has unfair rules for both women and men. Men can and absolutely do suffer from eating disorders and other mental health conditions linked to negative body image. However, women have uniquely been diluted to their appearance in the past and are still disproportionately impacted by negative body image, so that's who I'll mostly be talking about in this book—women.

Historically, the ideal female body has been dictated by men. In patriarchal societies, a woman's only hope to advance her status in life was to be deemed desirable by men—and therefore marriage material. In these societies, a woman's body was her only source of power. Of course, the men still held *ultimate* power since they're the ones who determined what was desirable.

Thankfully, a lot has changed for women. We can vote. We can own property. We can be leaders and scientists and educators and innovators and whatever the heck we want. Our lives don't have to be centered around making ourselves as desirable as possible so we can find a husband.

Yet we haven't fully shaken off our roots. We're still clinging to that antiquated, oppressive system that tells us *we are not enough as we are* and distorts the way we see ourselves. We're still spending our precious time, energy, and money chasing a made-up ideal shape. While we are no longer foot binding or wearing corsets, we have developed our own methods—things like waist trainers and detox shakes.

The Technological Contribution

Since their inception, television and film have communicated what a culture values. This is why the people portraying characters on a screen are typically beautiful (according to the current definition of beauty). Airbrushed magazine covers stare at us in checkout lines to remind us of what we're supposed to look like. It's everywhere we look. A survey conducted by the Florida House Experience found that 87% of women compare their bodies to those they see in the media. 50% of women compared their bodies unfavorably.

The meteoric rise of social media has amplified our exposure to cultural beauty standards. According to the PEW Research Center, 28% of Americans, and 48% percent of those aged 18 to 29, are online almost *constantly*.

With the astounding amount of time we spend online, it's seemingly impossible to not be affected by what we see. We will inevitably be shaped by people we follow online and the voices to which we subscribe. This is incredibly dangerous because many people online are hoping to exploit your insecurities for their gain.

Women, we're not off the hook. If men are the inventors of the ideal female form, we are the marketing team for it. Women perpetuate the myth that there is an ideal shape to be. Just scroll through Instagram and note the number of women selling a "new you". An *improved* version of yourself sold in the form of diet plans and weight loss products, waist-trainers, meal-replacement shakes, and fat-busting workout plans.

Each makes a lofty promise: *buy this and you will finally be good enough.* Of course, they don't deliver. But that doesn't stop us from buying the next thing anyway. Using our online presence like this is a disservice to other women and to ourselves.

Why Body Image Matters

Ladies, I don't think I need to tell you that negative body image among women is an epidemic. We all know it. By the time a girl is 17, research shows there is an 80% chance she will be unhappy with her body. Negative body image is a serious public health issue. It's a risk factor for a number of mental health conditions, including depression, anxiety, and eating disorders.

A study that followed 496 young girls for eight years found that by the time they were 20 years old, 5.2% of the girls had dealt with anorexia, bulimia, or binge eating disorder (Stice, Marti, Shaw, and Jaconis, 2010). A study that looked at over 2,400 people who were hospitalized for an eating disorder found that 97% had at least one co-occurring condition. 94% had co-occurring mood disorders, mostly major depression, and 56% had an anxiety disorder—obsessive-compulsive disorder, post-traumatic stress disorder, or an alcohol or substance use disorder (Tagay., Schlottbohm, Reyes-Rodriguez, Repic, & Senf, 2014). After opioid addiction, eating disorders have the highest mortality rate of all the mental health disorders (Chesney, Goodwin, & Fazel, 2014).

As the The National Eating Disorders Association (NEDA) puts it, "Eating disorders are serious conditions that can have a profound mental and physical impact, including death. This should not discourage anyone struggling—recovery is real, and treatment is available. Statistics on mortality and eating disorders underscore the impact of these disorders and the importance of treatment."

If you suspect you may be suffering from a mental health

disorder, please consider talking to a mental health professional. There is hope for you! Recovery is possible.

Even if you are never diagnosed with a mental health condition, a negative body image can still seriously affect your quality of life. Preoccupation with your body can distract you from important things like your relationships, education, work, spiritual life, and hobbies. Obsessing over having the perfect diet and fitness routine can hurt the overall well-being of your mental and emotional health. Pursuing a healthy body image is not a vain or trivial thing. It is a worthwhile goal that can improve your health and make your life better.

DIET CULTURE

◆ ◆ ◆

For far too many years, I convinced myself that light ice cream tastes the same as regular ice cream. You know the type. It's right next to the good stuff in the grocery store, masquerading as the real thing...but it is very much not. They have normal flavors like chocolate chip cookie, vanilla, and birthday cake, but those flavors should really be called "One Single Chocolate Chip Per Pint", "Almost-Sweet Concrete", and "Worst Birthday Ever."

After dinner, I'd pull out a fresh new container of light ice cream. I'd excavate a chunk of rock-hard flavored ice from a pint and think, "this is good, I am enjoying this." I would eat a carefully portioned serving and put the rest of it away, feeling unsatisfied yet so proud of my "willpower."

Many nights, I would end up sneaking back into the freezer and scraping out the very bottom of that pint. Still unsatisfied, I'd scavenge for whatever "treats" I had in the pantry, things like semi-sweet chocolate chips or peanut butter, and binge until I felt sick.

The labels on those colorful pints of light ice cream boast messages like "guilt-free" as if guilt is an ingredient mixed into other ice cream. Yet, they'd still left me feeling guilty and ashamed. Guilty that I had eaten more than a serving.

Ashamed of my desire for something that would actually satisfy my craving. I was convinced that the problem was me.

But the truth is, the problem wasn't me. I had been fooled. Clever marketing had exploited my insecurities. Now listen, I'm very aware that some people choose these alternative ice creams because of legitimate allergies or sensitivities. I'm not talking about that, because that was not me. What I was trying to do was convince myself that I didn't *need* real ice cream and that I didn't *want* real ice cream. But truthfully, I just believed I didn't *deserve* real ice cream. This is quintessential diet culture at work.

You have probably experienced diet culture before. It's that little voice that makes you feel guilty for eating a slice of cake. The headline shaming a celebrity for gaining weight, because *obviously* gaining weight is bad. It's also the panic you feel when you wonder if you're exercising enough to stay trim. It's that belief that nobody had to tell you to believe because the message is ubiquitous: thin is good, fat is bad. It's a system that values an "ideal" body shape above well-being and promotes dieting as a moral obligation, and it is *everywhere.*

Christy Harrison, MPH, RD, CDN, is the author of the book *Anti-Diet* and a leader in the weight-inclusive, anti-diet culture movement. Her definition of diet culture is widely accepted and referenced and I think it is the most helpful. She says:

"Diet culture is a system of beliefs that:

• Worships thinness and equates it to health and moral virtue, which means you can spend your whole life thinking you're irreparably broken just because you don't look like the impossibly thin 'ideal.'

• Promotes weight loss as a means of attaining higher status, which means you feel compelled to spend a massive amount of time, energy, and money trying to shrink your body, even though the research is very clear that almost no one can sustain intentional weight loss for more than a few years.

• Demonizes certain ways of eating while elevating others, which means you're forced to be hyper-vigilant about your eating, ashamed of making certain food choices, and distracted from your pleasure, your purpose, and your power.

• Oppresses people who don't match up with its supposed picture of 'health'...damaging both their mental and physical health" (Harrison, 2018).

You don't have to be on a diet to perpetuate diet culture. The way you think and talk about food, bodies, and health can reinforce the ideas that diet culture promotes. For example, if I look down on certain people and make assumptions about their health or character based on their size, I am participating in diet culture.

Diet culture can be sneaky. In the holistic health and wellness world, I see diet culture hiding behind health programs and "lifestyle changes" all the time. Even if a program claims not to be about weight loss, if it recommends cutting out major food groups, obsessively monitoring your food intake, or demonizing certain foods, diet culture has permeated it.

What is your "light ice cream"? How has diet culture snuck its way into your food choices? Start paying attention to your thoughts and behaviors and noticing how it affects you.

Weight Stigma

Diet culture has some serious consequences. Not only does it contribute to negative body image and a number of mental health issues, but it is also a *social justice issue.* Diet culture perpetuates weight stigma, which is discrimination on the basis of weight. This does all sorts of harm for fat people. Fat people are less likely to be hired or promoted at work. They are paid less. They are more likely to be bullied and excluded from social activities. Fat people receive a *far* lower quality of healthcare. This is what happens in a society where fat bodies are vilified and thought to be inferior.

Before I continue, please know that I'm using "fat" here as a neutral, descriptive word, as it has been reclaimed by the growing fat acceptance movement. If the use of that word makes you uncomfortable, ask yourself why (I'll go into this more later).

Also, know that I am limited in how much I am able to speak to weight stigma because I do not experience weight stigma myself. I am able to find clothes that fit me in stores, and doctors listen to my concerns. So, I have thin privilege. This does not necessarily mean my life has been easy or that I can't suffer from negative body image. It does not mean I haven't been hurt by diet culture—it just means I am not regularly discriminated against because of my size, so I benefit from a society that oppresses fat people. This is why I have consulted and included the words and thoughts of fat acceptance activists throughout this chapter.

Racist Roots

Diet culture is ultimately and firmly rooted in racism. People of color were the first people to face weight stigma and they continue to be the ones most affected by it today. Early in American history, weight was used to justify slavery as a way to separate white people from the "inferiorly gluttounous" black people, who tended to be heavier than white people

In *Fearing the Black Body,* Sabrina Strings explains that white people in the middle of the 18th century believed that "inferior races have no self-control…because of how interested they are in sex and food. This was really the beginning of linking what was considered an unruly type of fatness to Blackness."

Hanne Blank frames Strings' writings in this way: "Strings's central argument is quite simply this: the white West's loathing of fatness was built on and within a system of anti-Black racism. As European exploitation of Black people intensified in the seventeenth century, so did the accumulation of imagery, belief, stereotype, and story that served to distance white Europeans from the Black people they increasingly depended upon to generate their wealth."

"In time, this combined with eighteenth-century cultural aesthetics that developed within the English-speaking world that connected thinness with moral perfection and intellectual vigor, what Strings has named the 'ascetic aesthetic.' Jumping the pond to the newly-independent United States, the thin elongated paleness of the 'ascetic aesthetic' becomes a white American signature, a particularly fateful white supremacist abbreviation in a new nation whose economy grew on, and indeed could not have been forged without, the dehumanization and enslavement of Black people" (Nursing Clio, 2019).

Basically, the white western world's hatred of fatness started because of a hatred of Black people. This hatred spawned the belief that thinness correlates to moral and intellectual rightness. Though these ideas are no longer so covert, they still lie underneath, pressed into the foundation of our modern western culture.

These racist roots have deeply impacted the scientific and medical establishments. One example of this is the Body Mass Index (BMI), a value used to measure body fat. The BMI is widely accepted as a marker of health, but its origin story may surprise you. It was invented 200 years ago by Adolphe Quetelet, a Belgian astronomer, mathematician, statistician and sociologist (please note, he was not a physician).

Quetelet developed what is now known as the BMI based on the size and measurements of a group mostly made up of European men for the purpose of statistics. However, it has been used since the 1980s for the purposes of individual health care, though it was never created to be used in this way nor does it represent all people. To say the BMI is an inaccurate measurement of health is an understatement. It is a tool that does harm, especially to people of color and women, as it's freely used by doctors and health insurance companies to deny proper care.

Quetelet's contributions to scientific racism do not stop there. He co-founded the school of positive criminology, "which asserted the dangerousness of the criminal to be the only measure of the extent to which he was punishable. That positivist school laid the groundwork for criminologists like Cesare Lombroso, who believed that people of color were a separate species" (Your Fat Friends, 2019).

Science in the 1900s was rife with white supremacy, and the BMI continues to further the objective of white supremacists today. Weight continues to be the scapegoat used to explain health disparities between white people and minority populations, even though the true factors are more nuanced and complex. Studies are finding that social determinants of health such as access to healthcare, access to food, financial stability, environmental toxins, stress, and trauma are actually more consequential to health than diet or other health behaviors. To think an individual's health is only a direct result of their behavior is reductive and in come cases, racist.

If we claim to reject racism, we need to be willing to reject the racist notion that thin is better, even if (especially if) this idea benefits us. Body diversity is a wonderful thing—we are not all supposed to look the same. And there is certainly no such thing as an ideal size or shape.

Weight Stigma and Healthcare

"Okay, but what about health?" you might ask. "Isn't obesity an epidemic?" Well actually, studies are now finding that it's the weight stigma itself that explains the disparities in health between thin and fat people. Fat people have a higher chronic stress load because of the discrimination they face in our culture and in the medical establishment, which contributes to disease. Even the term "obesity" peddles a false narrative because it's based on the BMI, which we've already established is inaccurate and damaging. All that word does is pathologize a body size—it literally makes fatness a disease.

Lindo Bacon and Amee Severson have a great piece about weight stigma in Scientific American. It says, "When the American Medical Association declared obesity a disease, it overrode a recommendation by its own expert panel, which stated that correlations between 'obesity' and morbidity and mortality rates did not establish causality and there was concern that medicalizing 'obesity' would lead to further stigmatization and unnecessary treatment."

They continue, "'Obesity is the biggest threat to the health of our nation,' proclaims the chief of epidemiology at a major medical school on the Scientific American Observations blog. This all too common suggestion does far greater damage to public health than fat tissue itself. When the focus is on weight and body size, it's not 'obesity' that damages people. It's fear-mongering about their bodies that puts them at risk for diabetes, heart disease, discrimination, bullying, eating disorders, sedentariness, lifelong discomfort in their bodies, and even early death" (Bacon, 2019).

The medical establishment is full of weight stigma and fat bias. Many fat people avoid getting regular check-ups and screenings because they perceive their body weight to be a source of embarrassment in the healthcare setting. As a result, they often don't discover conditions until they are more advanced. When they do go in, they're met with a lower standard of care compared to thin people. Their concerns are dismissed and they're waved out the door with a weight loss prescription in hand (Phelan et al., 2015).

That doesn't sound like a concern for health to me. And that's because it's not—it's a concern for appearances, informed by the racist beliefs society holds about body size. Because we're supposed to be afraid of getting fat, we hate fat people. And because it's thought to be "unhealthy" to be fat, we're allowed to be afraid of getting fat and hate fat people for the sake of *health*. It's a just big ol' excuse we can hide our bigotry behind.

The research is clear: focusing on the weight does not make fat people healthier (Mann, Tomiyama, & Ward, 2015). In fact, it doesn't even make people thinner! The reign of diet culture and weight stigma has failed to reduce "obesity." Diets don't work. Most people who are actually able to lose weight on a diet gain it back—and sometimes more. But their physical health suffers because deprivation puts a lot of stress on the body and its systems. Their mental health also suffers because of negative body image, disordered thoughts, missing out on special events and social activities, and inevitable feelings of failure when the diet doesn't work.

Weight does not equal health, so don't be fooled into thinking you need to lose weight to be healthier. While "health" is more than physical, let's focus on physical health for a minute. Weight is a bad metric for health. We can't know anything about a person's health just by looking at them.

Metrics such as blood pressure, cholesterol, and blood sugar are more helpful than weight, but they are still imperfect; physicians disagree over what an optimal range is for each of them. They are just data points that need to be put into context.

How you feel is a better metric for physical health. Are you in pain? Do you have enough energy? How is your sleep? If you are in a state of well-being and your body is functioning properly, you do not need to lose weight to be healthy. If you are not in a state of well-being and your body is not functioning properly, losing weight will not make you healthy. If we are ever going to see an end to weight stigma, we need to stop focusing so much on how we look, and start caring more about how we feel.

Relationship With Food

Next time you go to the grocery store, you should skim the shelves to see how many times you see the words, "guilt-free," "light," "smart," or "skinny" on the packaging. These messages are soaked in diet culture. What these labels might as well be saying is, "Look at us! We're the responsible choice. You don't have to feel bad when eating these cookies because they won't make you fat!"

Diet culture uses tactics like these to ruin your relationship with food because it profits off of your disordered eating. It will find ways to make you distrust food.

Diet Culture Tactics

Creating rules around food is one tactic diet culture uses to sow distrust. Let's call these "food rules." Food rules are arbitrary guidelines that diet culture tries to enforce. They're things like: Don't eat after 7pm. Don't have more than one serving of fruit per day because it contains too much sugar. Only eat carbs before noon. Never eat gluten. Only eat desserts on the weekends. Only eat in an eight hour window. Instituting food rules keeps you from listening to your body's needs. Instead of listening to cues that you are hungry, you wait until you are "allowed" to eat. This creates distrust between you and your innate body wisdom.

We don't do this with any of our other bodily signals. Imagine having to pee and saying , "dang it, I can't pee until noon because I'm intermittent peeing today." That would be ridiculous, right?

Another tactic diet culture loves is making you believe food is a battle between good and evil—that certain foods (like broccoli) are good and other foods (like cookies) are bad. Food is not tied to morality. If you believe foods are good and bad, then you'll start to believe *you* are good or bad depending on what you eat. This is where guilt and shame enter your relationship with food.

There is no room for guilt and shame when it comes to eating because food does not contain or determine morality. Yes, some food is more nutrient-dense than other foods. Some animals are raised in more sustainable ways that benefit the planet and our bodies. Certain fats become rancid when they are mass-produced and heated at very high temperatures. There are studies that support the idea that certain ingredients in heavily-processed foods can have negative effects if consumed in large quantities. But these are just neutral facts.

Think about it this way…not everybody has access to the same quality of food. Does that mean a family who is living in poverty and can only afford to fuel their children with McDonalds for dinner is bad? Is that fast food meal bad? Certainly not. That meal is sustaining life.

"Good" is not reserved for those who are able to exclusively shop at Whole Foods and buy all organic, wild-caught, grass-fed food. Thinking of food as "good" or "bad" is just another way to heap shame and guilt on those who are less privileged.

How can you combat these diet culture tactics? How do you foster a healthy relationship with food? For that, we need to understand what food is *for*.

What Is Food For?

Every process in our body needs food to function. From our brains to our stomachs, from our muscles to our lungs, every single organ needs nutrients from food to work and keep us ticking. So yes, like every fitness guru on my Instagram feed loves to say, food is fuel. We need food to fuel life. But food is not only fuel. Food nourishes us in many ways.

When I was in high school, my family frequently got together for barbeques. I'm talking about my *whole* family: aunts, cousins, grandparents, neighbors, the whole shebang. Someone would grill up steak and sausages and chicken hearts and fill the entire backyard with a succulent, smoky haze.

When the meat was ready I'd hop out of the pool and make my way over to the folding table that held a myriad of treasures. Dripping wet, I'd make myself a plate: white rice with Brazilian vinaigrette on top, thinly sliced steak and sausage, farrofa (toasted cassava flour) to dip the meat in, and beans. I'd reach into a cooler and pull out a can of Guaraná, a mind-blowingly sweet Brazilian soda. As I write this, my salivary glands are turning into a cascading waterfall as I imagine the vinegary salsa perfectly complementing the warm rice and salty steak.

We still eat all of these things when we get together (and more—I could fill all these pages describing the wonders of Brazillian cuisine). This meal is deeply nourishing. Not only is it physically satisfying and filling, but it is something that I share with the people closest to me. It reminds me of my roots and my family's history. It is familiar and comforting and makes me think of the countless memories we've shared over a plate of churrasco and an ice-cold Guaraná .

Food is not just fuel, but also a means for social connection and engaging with your community. I've built many meaningful and fulfilling relationships over a cappuccino or plate of cookies. Food is a way to connect with your culture and your personal heritage. Sitting around the table with your family eating the same dishes your family has been making for generations is good for the soul.

Food holds cherished memories and can bring you emotional support. Food is for pleasure! It tastes and feels amazing and is one of the most simple and true joys in life. You are not "good" for refusing to partake in Grandma's pumpkin pie at Thanksgiving nor are you "bad" for eating a donut with your friends—or by yourself just because you feel like it!

Diet culture would have you ignore all of the other wonderful benefits of food. It would have you sacrifice pleasure, social connection, culture, and emotional support for thinness. To me, it's a no-brainer—it is not worth it. Honoring the many ways food can nourish us is the key to a healthy relationship with food.

"But What About Health?"

Nay-sayers love to defend dieting in the name of health. Because the medical establishment is so inundated with diet culture, it deems restrictive diets "healthy" because they would presumably make someone thinner. In doing so, they peddle the narrative that *thinner* means *better* and *healthier.* But restrictive diets are not actually healthier. Not only are they *not effective* at getting people to lose weight, but they can also cause physical and mental harm.

This is because *we cannot pursue health and weight loss at the same time*. They are inherently at odds, their goals fundamentally opposed. Sure, sometimes weight loss might happen as a side effect of healing, but other times, you might need to gain weight to heal. I have seen this in countless women: dieting and working out too much can leave a woman with terrible energy issues, horrible PMS, or sometimes no period altogether. In order to restore function to her endocrine system, she has to eat more food and might gain weight in the process. She has to break up with dieting and restricting to pursue health.

What Is a Healthy Diet?

A healthy diet is one where you have enough nutrients to keep you functioning. The key word there is "enough." We spend an awful lot of time and energy worrying about people overeating when in reality, undereating is just as harmful (if not more).

When you undereat, your body goes into survival mode. Your nervous system and endocrine system go into stress mode to keep you alive. Your immune system is compromised. Undereating will leave you cold, tired, sick, weak, and feeling horrible, but nobody seems all too concerned about that. "It's just the Keto Flu," they'll say. "At least you're losing weight," they'll add. "It's all worth it!" But is it? Or is it just unhealthy?

If you're not sure if your diet is healthy, ask yourself these questions:

- Am I eating enough to sustain myself?
- Do I feel deprived?
- Am I letting food nourish me in other ways too (emotion-

ally, socially, culturally, etc.)?

If your true concern is health, then you don't need to worry about dieting or losing weight. You can let food nourish every part of you. This is what it means to think holistically about health. It's about the whole person—every part, not just the body.

This is something I loved about the NTA's Nutritional Therapy Program. The NTA takes a holistic approach and is more focused on function than appearances. Its nutrition paradigm is more concerned with how you *feel* than how you *look*. It's concerned with things like: are you digesting your food? How's your energy? Are certain foods making you feel crummy? What foods are you missing that could help you feel more vibrant?

Before we move on, I want to note something here that is often overlooked: health is not an obligation. Pursuing health is not a prerequisite for worthiness or value as a human. Everyone deserves dignity, respect, compassion, and equal rights, regardless of health status.

Anti-Diet Movement

Thankfully, a shift is happening. Health providers are starting to break up with diet culture and the West's obsession with thinness. They've seen the harm it causes and they've had enough. It's called the Anti-Diet movement, and it opposes the oppressive system of diet culture.

Anti-Diet health providers teach people that weight loss is not a prerequisite for health. They maintain that you can be healthy and well at any size—and they've got the research to back it up. This is where people get caught up, because they've associated *weight loss* with *health* for so long. They wonder how a practitioner can be Anti-Diet and not anti-health.

Anti-Diet practitioners are not at all anti-health. Anti-Diet practitioners are very much about health and helping people pursue health-promoting behaviors. The difference is that they maintain a more inclusive and holistic approach to wellness. For example, they offer nutrition counseling for medical conditions like hypothyroidism without throwing weight loss advice into the mix.

Two frameworks some Anti-Diet practitioners use in their practices are Intuitive Eating and Health At Every Size® (HAES), and both are very helpful. Intuitive Eating, an approach started by Evelyn Tribole and Elyse Resch, is all about rejecting diet rules and honoring your hunger cues.

The ten principles of Intuitive Eating are:

1. Reject the Diet Mentality: Stop dieting and start getting angry at diet culture.

2. Honor Your Hunger: Eat when you're hungry to rebuild trust with your body.

3. Make Peace with Food: Give yourself unconditional permission to eat.

4. Challenge the Food Police: Get rid of the unreasonable rules diet culture has created.

5. Discover the Satisfaction Factor: Enjoy your food.

6. Feel Your Fullness: Honor your body's signals that tell you you're full.

7. Cope with Your Emotions with Kindness: Develop coping skills.

8. Respect Your Body: Accept your body as it is.

9. Movement—Feel the Difference: Focus on how working out makes you feel.

10. Honor Your Health—Gentle Nutrition: Eat foods that honor your health, taste good, and make you feel good.

Dietitians around the world have adopted Intuitive Eating and found it to be a happier, healthier way to eat.

HAES, pioneered by Dr. Lindo Bacon, is a scientifically-backed health care approach that does not focus on weight. It promotes healthy lifestyle habits (movement, nutrient-dense foods, nurturing connections, etc.) and accepts size diversity —because both can live in harmony.

Weight loss is a multi-billion dollar industry that *profits off of you hating your body*. Rejecting diet culture is counter-cultural, challenging, and brave.

Dieters

I had a hunch my now-husband was going to propose weeks before he actually did. I had a hunch because he is a terrible liar. "Sure, I'll join you in Miami for a special date for no reason…" He gifted me a dress to wear on this date, something he had done several times before. But this time was different, because I knew this would be the dress I would be wearing when he proposed. I knew I would be photographed in this dress and that I would have to look at those pictures for the rest of my life.

Sadly, I was disappointed by how I looked in the dress. I liked the flowy, yellow dress, I just decided the halter neckline accentuated my "chicken fat" (you know, that thing under your armpits called SKIN) more than I could bear.

That's when I did something I would regret for the rest of my life: I told him I couldn't wear the dress. I looked this sweet, thoughtful man in the face and told him I would not wear the dress he carefully selected for me for our proposal—all because of my insecurity. This is what diet culture does to us; it hijacks even our most precious moments and makes them about our bodies. I'll note, I was at the thinnest I had ever been in my adult life, and still, I did not feel like I was thin enough. I was so ashamed of my "imperfections" that I could not even enjoy such a special gift.

I vividly remember what it was like to be that girl, and I have so much compassion for her. If you chose to pursue weight loss or have body physique goals, know that I hold no judgment toward you. I have been there and I get it. It's your body and you can choose to do whatever you want with it.

My beef is with diet culture, not with dieters. I've called out the health and social ramifications of diet culture, but that doesn't mean I hold judgement for people who diet. I do, however, have a couple of questions. Dieters, are you participating in diet culture because you want to, or because you feel like you have to maintain a certain size? If it's the latter, then maybe you have been shaped by diet culture more than you realize. Maybe it's time you break up with diet culture too.

BODY POSITIVITY: A FLAWED SOLUTION

◆ ◆ ◆

When I was in college I started noticing a subtle shift. Different body types started showing up on the photo displays at Target and on mannequins at the mall. Plus-size models were all the rage and happily flaunted their curves on magazine covers and strutted their stuff in perfume commercials. What I was noticing was a new wave of the body positivity movement, which was borne out of the fat awareness movement around 2012.

At the time, I was still deeply entrenched in diet culture, so I did not buy into the whole thing. Sure, it was cool to see models who looked more like me—I was almost encouraged by it. But deep down, I still believed they were lucky to be there and that people didn't actually believe they were as attractive as their size 2 counterparts.

I think I wanted to believe they deserved to be there too, but my disordered view of myself kept me from appreciating what was happening. Deep down I believed that their bodies, just like my body, still needed to apologize for taking up space.

Right Direction

Early on, the movement was about empowering plus-size women—according to the fashion industry, women who wear over a size 18—to love their bodies.

It promoted the idea that every single body is beautiful and worth celebrating, and sought to normalize things that were traditionally thought of as flaws or "un-ladylike"—things like cellulite, body hair, and menstruation.

In the early years of the movement, "...it was a somewhat-diverse, social-media-based community celebrating self-love and radical self-acceptance of fat bodies of all races, with early prominent figures in the movement including Jes Baker, Sonya Renee Taylor, Jessamyn Stanley and Kivan Bay. (Yeboah, 2020)"

These women represented those who are most often swept to the side, and their voices were powerful and moving. Their ideas were radical and revolutionary at the time. They challenged the standards that were expected of women and the oppressive forces behind them. They rejected diet culture. And their message spread like wildfire.

We started seeing more representation of plus-size bodies in fashion and in the media. Shows like *Euphoria* starred plus-size protagonists who were not relegated to the stereotypical fat characters we were used to seeing in the early 2000s.

Aerie launched their "AerieReal" campaign where the models were not photoshopped or retouched. Heck, even Barbie started coming out in different sizes and colors. The body positivity movement did a lot of good.

Flaws

But something changed and the movement was hijacked. Body positivity was commodified and watered down into a way to increase profits by appealing to the plus-size demographic. All of a sudden, every brand in the country had a "love yourself" program or product or campaign, and few of them felt sincere.

On social media, hundreds of new body positivity influencers emerged, most of them white and "acceptably fat," meaning they have white or European features, an hourglass shape, and a small waist. This created a new standard of beauty, one that once again left out the most marginalized people.

This new standard left behind the people who suffer most at the hands of weight stigma and racial bias. Once again, fat people of color are denied a seat at the table. There is no room because every seat is occupied by profit-seeking brands and well-meaning, "acceptably fat" white women.

Let me clarify—I am not asserting that I think white, "acceptably fat" women should not be involved in body activism work. What I *am* saying is that when we are fighting oppression, we must consult and amplify the voices of those who are actually oppressed, so we don't prioritize our own privileged experiences (preaching to myself here too). I think the body positivity movement has failed to do this well.

While the movement challenged unrealistic standards of beauty, it failed to challenge why there is *any* standard of beauty. While it has sought to restore our collective relationships with our bodies, it has not addressed why we have such broken views of ourselves in the first place.

The body positivity movement does not reject the patriarchal belief that a woman's value is tied to her appearance. So while it opens up the gates for more women to be considered beautiful, the gates lead directly into the belly of the patriarchy.

Why continue to feed into society's obsession with beauty? Why not bust the whole thing down? I think body positivity has done a lot of good for a lot of people. The fact that girls who do not meet our culture's standard of beauty can see themselves on the big screen and in magazines is a big deal. It's wonderful that so many social media influencers are being transparent about their "flaws" and encouraging people to love their bodies.

But what if we don't have to love our bodies? Which, I might add, is often an impossible task because of the culture we're surrounded with. There's a better way to combat body image issues and diet culture, and it doesn't come with a new standard of beauty.

What Is Love?

When you hear "love your body," what do you think? When some people use it, they mean, "I think I look good," but that definition of love is pretty weak.

Let me put it this way: I love my husband. And sure, I think he looks good. He's a cutie pie—and that was part of what initially attracted me to him. But that was infatuation, not true love. I love him *way* more now than I did when we were a couple of heart-eyed teenagers. My love for him is not just a feeling—feelings waver far too much. It is unconditional and secure. I accept and respect all that he is and I earnestly care for him.

That's what it means to love, and that's how we can love our bodies. Loving your body is not about thinking you look good all the time, it's about knowing that your body is worthy of acceptance, respect, and care no matter what you look like. When your body image is rooted in a neutral space without any pressure on you to love how you look, you can spend more energy on *actually* loving your body.

THE PRACTICE OF BODY NEUTRALITY

❖ ❖ ❖

I married my college sweetheart in 2019 in a dreamy, historic Miami estate. It was a warm February day filled with big hugs, weepy loved ones, cuban food, and dancing. Then, we honeymooned in Bali and moved in together and filled our first home with new furniture and plates and towels. It was pretty sweet. 2019 was a high point in my life, but health-wise, it was the year I tanked.

Six months after my wedding, I couldn't ignore the signs anymore. I was tired. Not "tired" in the way that every adult is tired, but tired in a something-is-wrong way. I felt too tired to do things I once loved, even after exceptionally long nights of sleep. I couldn't move weight at the gym like I used to and traveling up the stairs became laborious. Even the smallest of tasks, like answering an email, felt overwhelming. I no longer recognized the sluggish, anti-social person I had become. I eventually realized I needed professional help.

Suspecting a hormonal imbalance, I asked my doctor to do some comprehensive hormone testing. We discovered a number of imbalances, including very low levels of DHEA and Cortisol, two hormones produced by the adrenal glands that impact energy levels.

How did I get here? The short answer is stress. The long answer, though, reveals that diet culture was largely involved in the demise of my endocrine health. I stressed my body out too much in the 10 months I was engaged. Sure, there were the normal stressors: planning a wedding, working full-time, managing my social life. But I also bought into the societal pressure to look super "fit" (aka, thin) on my wedding day.

At that point, I had already been doing high-intensity workouts several times per week and meticulously keeping track of my diet. I stepped it up even more. I ate less calories, tracked each macronutrient, worked out more, slept less to accommodate those demands, and drank more coffee to keep myself going. All of that, for 10 months straight, really did me in. My body said "you WILL slow down…whether you like it or not."

I did not like it—but I also had no choice. Today, I am still in a period of healing my adrenal glands (and my entire endocrine system since hormones are all connected, so dysfunction in one area causes dysfunction in other areas—hello, PMS and hypothyroidism). I stopped doing intense workouts and started walking and practicing yoga. I switched from coffee to matcha. Most importantly, I stopped dieting. This is the piece that has made the greatest difference for me.

I was trying to force my body into a shape it was never supposed to be. Sure, I was the smallest I had ever been in my adult life on my wedding day, but at what cost? I was also putting a high load of stress on my body by withholding the nutrients and calories it really needed.

In letting go of weight loss, I learned what health actually is. For the first time in my life, I was able to truly focus on nurturing and nourishing my body, mind, and soul. In this period of healing, which again, I am still in and may be in for a while,

I have gained weight. While I know this is normal and both a good and necessary part of my healing, it was a hard thing to accept at first.

My identity had been tied to being a "fit" health nut. What would people think about my weight gain? Would they think I wasn't healthy or fit anymore? This train of thought led me to a very important question: why do we make assumptions about health based on outward appearances?

This led me to the Anti-Diet movement. This led me to HAES and Intuitive Eating. In these spaces I found practitioners who affirmed the convictions that had been stirring in my mind. This also led me to the movement that would become my biggest step toward liberation: body neutrality.

What Is Body Neutrality?

Body neutrality is the practice of accepting and respecting your body exactly as it is because you have inherent worth regardless of your outward appearance. Unlike body positivity, it does not try to expand the door to beauty. In fact, it does not grapple with beauty at all! It rejects society's complete and utter obsession with appearances and recenters our eyes on our inner, inherent worth.

Body neutrality gave me a new way to relate to my body. I did not have to love or hate my body—my body could simply be. That, my friends, is what shook me up. That is what made me realize I had struck gold when I bumped into this philosophy. I could have peace with my body. I didn't have to feel any particular type of way about it. It didn't have to take up an absurd amount of space in my mind. What freedom!

Anne Poirier, BS, CSCS, CIEC coined the term "body neutrality" when she created a body neutrality workshop in 2015. Since then, it has been adopted by activists like *The Good*

Place actress Jameela Jamil.

Jameela's interviews were one of my first exposures to the movement. She fearlessly calls out celebrities for using their influence to promote harmful diet products like skinny teas and waist trainers. She created iWeigh, an organization that promotes radical inclusivity for those who don't fit into society's made-up standards. She represents the movement well because she embraces her body, yet she knows she is *more than a body.*

Body neutrality is the practice of accepting and respecting your body because of your inherent worth, but what does that really mean? Let's break down the concept a little more.

Acceptance

To accept your body is to peaceably inhabit it. You must wave the white flag and concede to the forces that compel you to wage war against your body. Accepting your body means holding the truth that *your body is exactly as it is supposed to be* right now, in this moment, and that is a good thing.

Diet culture will have you do anything but accept your body —it will tell you to change and fight and shrink and deny. Body neutrality says, "put down the weapons." Own your space, own your body. It is a part of you, and it's not your enemy. So you can make peace with it.

When you peaceably inhabit your body, you don't have to think about it that much. You don't have to stand in front of a mirror and try to love every body part. You don't have to stand in front of a mirror and lament the parts you hate. You can just *be.* Your reflection becomes a neutral force in your life—something that just *is.* The same way your voice just is. The same way your hair color just is.

Respect

Your body is the vehicle by which you experience the world. It carries you through life, each and every day, so it deserves your respect. Respecting your body means treating it with dignity by meeting its needs. The body needs many things: food, water, sunlight, and movement to name a few. But we all need these things in different amounts, in different forms, and at different times. We have other unique needs, too. Our needs may also change throughout our lives as our situations change.

We are all biologically different. We all come with our own set of genetics, lifestyles, stressors, and life phases. That means w*hat works for me may not work for you.* There is no one-size-fits-all way to eat or move. Anyone that tells you otherwise is trying to sell you something.

Diet culture distorts our idea of what body respect looks like. It makes us think we are doing a good thing by restricting food and convinces us that more exercise is always better, which is not always the case. Truly caring for your body means giving your body the nutrients it needs and participating in movement that feels good. It means not always trying to be in a caloric deficit that will leave your body cold, tired, and stressed. It means giving your body the rest it needs and not forcing yourself to do intense workouts that wipe you out for the rest of the day.

When you're on a diet, you are chained down by food rules. Even if you're not "on a diet" but you're still believing the messages of diet culture, you're living in bondage. It is only when you choose to respect your body first and foremost that you'll be free to honor it—to listen to it and give it what it needs.

Worth

I know not everybody who reads this will share my faith, but

I believe each person was deliberately created by God. I believe that you have value and worth, given to you by a loving creator. This worth does not need to be earned and it cannot be taken away. It is yours!

Nothing you have done or could ever do can take that away. You are valuable and special. You are the only one of you and you have a purpose to live out on this earth. This value does not come from what you do and it certainly doesn't come from what you look like. Society perpetually values women for *only their looks*. This creates an insulting, watered-down version of who you are and why you matter.

I understand that this is easy to say and incredibly difficult to live out. But if our worth is inherent, and not earned, everything is different. Worth is not something you need to chase, because you already have it. That is the key to unlocking body acceptance and respect. Because you are already worthy, *you can accept and respect every part of you*, including your body, as something of value.

How to Practice

Body neutrality is something that you practice, not a place you arrive. You don't wake up one morning and decide, "I am body neutral" and that's that. You have to wake up every day and practice it. This may feel clunky at first but after a while, it'll start to feel as natural as breathing.

I'm going to give you three strategies for practicing body neutrality in your everyday life. The strategies will relate to your thoughts, words, and actions around your body. The first strategy is about how you talk to yourself, the second is about how you talk to others, and the third is about how you care for yourself.

These simple but practical methods have been so helpful for me as I practice body neutrality. They are tried and true and passed on to you with care. I promise I'm not going to give you a ton of things to add to your to-do list because I'm sure you have enough. But I will present you with some ideas that I want you to sit with. Take your time, let them challenge you, and take them with you into those vulnerable moments when you're grappling with your body image. I hope you find they are protective in those moments. I hope they are tools you can use to make peace with your body.

STRATEGY 1: SELF-TALK

◆ ◆ ◆

Some days, I still have negative thoughts about my body. When that happens, I have to interrogate my thoughts to see what's going on. Just the other day I looked in the mirror first thing in the morning and was surprised and disappointed by my reflection.

My body has changed a lot in the last year and I am still not used to the way I look right now, and that morning I felt really crummy about myself. My initial thought was, "I used to look so much better than this." I went about my day believing that, and it put me in a horrible, cranky mood (isn't it wild how negative body image is able to hijack our mood and attitude like that?).

I had to ask myself where this bad mood was coming from. So I traced it back to that morning and that initial thought I was believing about my body. When I looked further, I realized that initial thought revealed some other nasty stuff underneath.

The initial thought was, "I used to look better." I was believing my value had decreased because I gained weight, my husband wouldn't think I was attractive anymore, and that my body is not supposed to change—none of which I actually believe. Digging to that place allowed me to root myself in what I actually know to be true—that my value is not based on my weight, my husband's affection is not conditional, and my body is *supposed* to change.

Negative body image is not a body problem, so there is not a body solution. Changing your body will not fix your body image. It is a problem of the mind, so that's where the change needs to happen. This is hard work, because it is hard to change your mind. It is hard to change your beliefs. This work requires a lot of patience and practice.

Self-talk is a powerful tool. Katie Byron has published extensive writings on this work. She writes, "self-inquiry allows you access to the wisdom that already exists within you. It gives you the opportunity to realize the truth for yourself. Truth doesn't come or go; it's always here, always available to the open mind. If I can teach you anything, it is to identify the stressful thoughts that you're believing and to question them, to get still enough so that you can hear your own answers." She cautions against believing our own stories, because our own stories often lead to suffering and a lot of times, we know they're not true!

There is no wrong or right in this process. You can investigate your thoughts without judgement. Katie Bryon is not interested in eliminating negative thoughts or manipulating yourself into a delusional state of happiness. She encourages not suffering *unnecessarily* over something that isn't true, getting to a place that is real, and "loving what is." Your feelings are valid and sometimes we need to grieve the fact that our bodies are changing. Self-talk will not take away that grief, nor should it, but it can help you reframe your thoughts in a healthy way. I'm going to break down this type of self-talk into three steps.

Step 1: Notice

Step one is to notice your thoughts. This may feel strange if you've never done this before. When you're having a bad body image day, pay attention to what you're thinking. You might notice some physical discomfort that indicates something is off: tight neck or shoulders, tightness in your chest, sweaty palms, etc. Take a moment to be curious; investigate this discomfort. Identify what you're thinking but don't *judge* your thoughts—just notice them. It might even help to write them down.

Your initial thoughts about your body are important because they're actually your initial assumptions, or things you're accepting as truth in the moment. They could sound like:

- "I hate my body"
- "I look fat in this picture"
- "I can't pull off this outfit"
- "I should lose a few pounds"
- "I need to fit into that dress"
- "I wish I looked like *her*"
- "I am ugly"
- "I am ashamed of my body"
- "I am not pretty enough"
- "I am not thin enough"
- "I am just not enough"

If you're thinking, "gosh, I have thought every single one of these" then I am right there with you, sister. But here's the good news: we don't have to just accept these assumptions! This brings me to the next step.

Step 2: Investigate

Next, investigate your thoughts. Challenge those initial assumptions and ask yourself these questions:

1. Why am I believing this thought?

2. How do I feel when I believe it?

3. Who would I be without this thought?

Do this for each thought you have about your body that makes you upset. You can write this down too, but it's not necessary—you can answer these questions in your head. Your investigation might lead you to some deeply-rooted beliefs that you didn't even know you were holding onto. Those beliefs might be what led to that initial assumption. You might find that these beliefs don't align with your core values. What then? What do you do with your findings? That's the next step.

Step 3: Affirm

Lastly, find a way to reframe your initial assumption so that it aligns with your core values. You can do this by affirming what you know to be true and bringing that thought back to a place of acceptance, respect, and worth.

Here are twenty affirmations you can bring yourself back to. You can use one of these or make up your own:

- My worth is not determined by my weight

- My worth is not determined by my appearance
- I deserve to be present and not worried about my appearance
- My body is not the most important thing about me
- My body is going to change throughout my life, and that's okay
- My body keeps me alive everyday and allows me to experience the world
- My body deserves to be cared for
- I don't need to change my body
- I don't have to try to fit into any standard of beauty
- I don't need to feel guilty for eating
- I don't have to feel or look attractive to accept and respect my body
- I don't have to feel or look attractive to be happy
- I don't have to feel attractive to live my best life
- I can take care of my body even when I don't feel particularly good about it
- I can reject diet culture and its lies
- I am so much more than just a body
- I am allowed to take up space
- I am unique and special
- I am worthy of love

- I am valuable

These affirmations build resiliency. Speak them to yourself. Write them in your journal, on your mirror, memorize your favorites, and keep them in your pocket for a rainy day. Be ready to notice your thoughts, investigate them, and meet them with an affirmation you know to be true.

And these things *are* true and *do* apply to you—every single one. Sometimes I struggle to believe that for myself. My insecurities rub up against them and make them hard to really believe and live out. But in those moments, it helps me to "fake it until I make it," because I don't like who I am when I'm living like I don't believe them. I am a much more joyful, satisfied person when I am living like they are true.

You don't have to do this perfectly. It's hard to change your assumptions—it's messy and it takes time. But in my experience, it is possible and it is life changing. Practice has helped me a ton. The more I dwell on these affirmations and others like them, the more resilient I am to those nagging thoughts that tell me I'm not enough, and the more equipped I am to disarm them. Armed with truth, I am ready to overcome my bad body image days and make peace with my body.

Practice

Alright, now let's practice some self-talk using the three steps I gave you.

Step 1: Let's say I sensed some tension in my neck while shopping for a new outfit for a holiday party, and I suddenly feel like I'm on the verge of tears. I'm growing more and more frustrated as I'm trying on dresses because nothing in my usual size is fitting. I stop and *notice* my thoughts. I notice that the initial assumption floating around my mind is, "I can't believe I let myself gain this much weight—I'm a failure."

Step 2: I *investigate* this thought further. I ask myself three questions and they reveal there's more going on beneath the surface.

• *Why am I believing this thought?* Because everywhere I look I see messages and signs that I'm supposed to be thin, and if I'm not, I've "let myself go."

• *How do I feel when I believe it?* Horrible about myself. Like I'm a worthless failure that needs to get her act together.

• *Who would I be without this thought?* A lot happier. Free to enjoy shopping and picking out a beautiful outfit. Free to enjoy the party instead of fretting about how I look.

Step 3: Now I'm going to counter my assumption with an affirmation I know to be true. I'm going to use what I learned in step two to bring me back to a place of acceptance, respect, and worth. I choose to *affirm* these truths: I do not have to be thin, I am not a failure, and I have not let myself go—I know that not dieting is the best thing for my mental and physical health and I care for my body in the ways that are best for me. These affirmations help me to relax and allow me to continue shopping without being panicky about my weight. No tears in the dressing room today!

I will add: sometimes negative body image thoughts will hit at inconvenient times when you can't go through these steps. If you're running out the door because you're late for work, with a group of people, or in the middle of a movie, you might not be able to pause and do some serious self-talk. In those instances, what I do and what I recommend you do is you capture that thought and save it for later. Imagine you're literally putting it in a bubble, and later on when you have a few moments to spare, pop the bubble and go through the steps. If you think you'll forget what it is, write a little note in your phone.

We constantly make up stories about ourselves. Sometimes, these stories hurt us and put us in a really bad mood. You can't control what other people think or what culture says about women or health or bodies, but you can control what stories you believe about *yourself*. Self-talk allows us to do that. It helps us capture our assumptions and make a choice: accept it, or reframe it in a helpful, empowering way.

STRATEGY 2: NEUTRAL LANGUAGE

❖ ❖ ❖

"Words are seeds that do more than blow around. They land in our hearts and not the ground. Be careful what you plant and careful what you say. You might have to eat what you planted one day." I love this little saying by an unknown author because it means more every time I read it.

Words have this way of not only *reflecting* what our hearts believe, but also *influencing* what our hearts believe. Words are currency. The words we say and accept from others are votes for what we think the world should be like. They're one of the few agents for change we are afforded in this life. And they're a resource we should treasure, because of the big impact they can have.

The second strategy for practicing body neutrality is using neutral words to talk about food and bodies. Mimicking diet culture language about food is harmful. Speaking disparagingly about bodies—yours or someone else's—is harmful. It harms not only yourself, but also all the other ears listening around you.

Food

Let's tackle food first. Here are some non-neutral words that may cause harm:

• **"Clean eating"**: This implies there are dirty foods. Unless you are talking about literal dirt because it was just picked or fell on the floor. In that case, rinse it with soap and water and voilà, clean food. Using "clean" and "unclean" to talk about food causes unnecessary fear that can lead to disordered eating.

• **"Healthy"**: This is a loaded term. Diet culture loves to use health as an excuse to police people's eating habits. Health is nuanced and multifactorial, so no food can be labeled "healthy" all the time. If I've been outside doing physical labor all day, coming home and eating greens and cauliflower is not what's healthy for me at that moment. Sometimes diet culture is sneaky and tries to brand itself as "wellness." Companies and individuals will claim they're not promoting weight loss; they'll claim they're just promoting "getting healthy." But don't be fooled. They've co-opted the word "healthy" to mean "thin." Their "lifestyle change" is actually a disordered relationship with food and your body.

• **"Unhealthy"**: Health is complicated. It's determined by a number of factors, including genetics, socioeconomic status, stress load, trauma, environment, etc. To act as though lifestyle habits like diet and exercise are the only things that determine health is reductive and irresponsible.

• **"I'm being good"**: Food does not have morality and it does not determine your morality. You do not need to follow any food rules. Don't eat at night? Never eat carbs? Only one sweet per week? Those are all arbitrary food rules. And they are completely made up.

- **"I'm so bad"**: See the last point. You are allowed to enjoy food! You are allowed to enjoy it without any guilt, shame, or regret.

- **"Cheat meal"**: When you allow access to foods you typically restrict, it's easy to overeat past a comfortable point. You may even binge eat, and then feel physically sick and guilty afterward. This language implies what you are eating is bad, dirty, and wrong, which is false.

- **"Fattening"**: This is a fat-phobic word that reinforces the lie that the worst thing you could possibly be is fat.

- **"Junk food"**: What you consider junk may be all some people have access to. All foods provide some sort of nutrients. They may not be abundant in micronutrients (Vitamin C, Vitamin E, Magnesium, etc.), but all foods have macrominerals (fats, proteins, and carbohydrates), which we need to stay alive. That means "empty calories" is a myth too.

Here are some neutral words you can use to describe food instead:

- **"Nutrient-dense"** or **"energy-dense"**: Some foods have more nutrients than others. Some foods have more calories (energy) than others. You can describe foods in this way without attaching morality to them.

- **"Good"**: Good food is food that you like. As in, "wow, this lobster ravioli is really good!"

- **"Bad"**: Bad food is food that you don't like or food that has expired.

- **"Delicious"**, **"Satisfying"** or **"Fun"**: It's okay to eat yummy foods! Food is not just fuel. It is also for social connection, emotional support, cultural expression, and pleasure. Food is not only a basic need, but it is also one of the most basic pleasures we have here on earth.

• **"Sweet"**, **"Sour"**, **"bitter"**, **"salty"**, or **"umami"**: Notice the five basic tastes and different combinations they can make. Cooking is a craft and food is magical. There is so much you can do with it!

Bodies

Society has a lot of positive or neutral words for thin bodies: skinny, svelte, model-like, lean, tiny. But, we don't really know what to say about non-thin bodies (or we just don't care). Words like "larger-bodied" or "bigger" insinuate that those bodies are not normal and deviate from what is acceptable. They are an attempt at political-correctness that actually end up alienating people. Larger than what? Bigger than who?

Fat

So what word do members of the fat acceptance movement prefer? Fat. Does that word make you uncomfortable? That's probably because of how often you hear it used as an insult or a bad word. You probably hear people complain that they "look fat" or "feel fat." "Fat" has such a negative connotation because diet culture tells us the worst thing in the world we could possibly be is fat. But, many fat women have reclaimed the word for themselves. Writer and activist Your Fat Friend has an abundance of compelling work out there on this topic, and I have learned a lot from her. She writes:

"Do not rush to correct fat friends who name their own bodies for themselves, using the words that fit their experience. Recognize that a fat person daring to name their own body is an act of growth and that when you correct us, you stunt it. It is also an act of rebellion, and when you silence it, you silence us. Remember that your comfort does not take precedence over our autonomy. Do not rush to soothe and center your own discomfort by insisting 'sweetie, no! You're not fat!' Let us say our own names for ourselves. Just say fat."

"Do not add caveats and qualifiers. Do not say 'fat but healthy,' 'fat but working on it,' 'fat, but not, like, 400 pounds,' or 'fat but happy.' If you're taking a stand for fat people, take a stand for all of us. Do not limit our humanity by limiting who among us you will accept. Just say fat."

Recognize that your discomfort with the word may be because of your own internalized fat-phobia and the influence of diet culture. The "politically correct" terms you use are probably not what fat people actually prefer, and these terms may be doing harm to fat people in your life.

Words like "overweight" and "obese" are not unoffensive medical terms, either. Many fat people find these words hurtful and offensive, or even violent. They are words that have been used to declare war on their bodies—words that excuse medical negligence and prevent them from receiving the healthcare they need. "Overweight" and "obese" are terms that were popularized by the BMI, which we have already established is a complete farce.

"Curvy," "big-boned," "fluffy," and other similar words are just ways to avoid saying "fat." The reality is, we live in a fat-phobic world, so you might still be believing that fat is bad. We are literally terrified of getting fat. I think a lot of women I know would rather be hit by a bus than gain weight. Contrary to what our culture believes, "fat" is not bad. It is a neutral, descriptive word, and we don't need to be afraid of it.

Keep in mind that fat people are not a monolith—they don't all think the same. You may encounter someone who does not like the word "fat" and prefers other descriptive words. In those cases, let them take the lead. Respectfully call this person what they would prefer to be called; choose their comfort over yours. This is how we can uplift marginalized communities.

Don't Say Anything at All

Are you still confused about how to talk about bodies? The good news is you don't ever have to talk about someone else's body! In fact, most of the time, it's best not to. And I'm not just talking about fat bodies.

We love to praise thin bodies. We love to celebrate weight loss as if it's the greatest human achievement (e.g. Adele suddenly appeared on every tabloid after she lost weight). This is reckless and dangerous because we have no idea what people are going through or how they lost weight. Did they lose weight because they're suffering a terrible loss and keep forgetting to eat? Have they developed a severe eating disorder?

Even if it's not something like that, think about what you are saying to someone when you celebrate their weight loss. You are saying that they are better off now, that they are more valuable now that they are thin. You may be reinforcing their greatest insecurity that they are more worthy and loved when they are thin, and thus, less worthy and loved when they are not. What happens if and when they gain the weight back? Studies show an overwhelming majority do.

What if we're not even talking about weight. Think about how frequently we talk about appearances. Little girls grow up hearing "you're so pretty, cute dress, go brush your hair." Girlfriends hype eachother up like, "you look SO hot." There is nothing inherently wrong with that, but we need to carefully consider what we're communicating with our compliments.

If the first and only thing we comment on is someone's appearance, *we're communicating that what they look like is the most noteworthy thing about them.* I love it when my husband tells me he thinks I'm beautiful. I want him to find me physically attractive! But I also want to be reminded that that's not the only thing he values about me. I want him to affirm my character, my ideas, my strength, my jokes. I want to be affirmed for the other things I bring to the table, for the things that make me, me.

Looks change. Bodies change. If you really want to encourage and uplift someone in your life, compliment something that lasts. Let little girls be more than pretty. Tell them they are bright and clever and special. Let your girlfriends know they make your life better. Remind your partner that your love and affection is not based on their appearance. If you have nothing body neutral to say, maybe you don't need to say anything at all.

STRATEGY 3: SELF-CARE

❖ ❖ ❖

Body neutrality is a framework that impacts your thoughts and your words, but also your actions. The first two strategies were more about accepting your body as it is. This third strategy is about respecting your body.

When you know that your worth is fixed, and you don't need to work against, manipulate, or change your body, you can truly care for it. Shame and disgust don't make for good motivators for self-care, which is why letting those go and respecting our bodies makes such a profound impact on our wellbeing.

The beautiful thing is that this strategy is a great one to practice even if you're not feeling particularly body neutral. Even when you feel really horrible about your body and are struggling to practice self-talk and neutral language, you can still *take care* of your body. This third strategy is most effective when it precedes the first two, but if you have to start here, it might make the first two easier. Remember, body neutrality is something you practice, not something you master or achieve.

I'm going to give you very practical ways to practice self-care in a body neutral way. It's important that you know self-care can look however you need it to look. I'm not going to recommend specific foods or protocols or plans because that would not be helpful—we are unique and complicated creatures who need wildly different things. As you practice body neutrality, and treat your body as an ally and not an enemy, you will become more aware of what you need. There are a few basic things we all need.

Nourishment

Food is a basic need. We've been eating all our lives, yet nutrition can seem like the most confusing thing in the world. I get it, and I'm with you. The internet is full of conflicting messages when it comes to nutrition. But I'll let you in on a little secret: most people don't know what they're talking about. A lot of people are just trying to sell you something or are ill-informed and rely on bad science to back up their claims. Some people think they're qualified to give nutrition advice just because they're "fit."

Nutrition science is nuanced and complicated, and there are few big, sweeping recommendations that apply to all people. If you are concerned about your diet, suspect you have allergies or sensitivities, or just want some additional support, please seek out a qualified practitioner, not an influencer with no training.

I am an NTP (Nutritional Therapy Practitioner), but I am not *your* NTP, so I cannot make any specific recommendations for you. But I will offer you three pieces of self-care advice. First, eat regularly. Make sure you are getting enough food every single day. Secondly, eat a variety of food—lots of different produce and animal products and grains. That's the best way to get in a variety of all the different nutrients we need to function well. Thirdly, eat foods that will nourish your body, mind, and soul (i.e. eat foods that you love!). Eat foods that fill you up and make you feel good, bring you comfort and pleasure, and connect you to your loved ones and culture.

How you do these three things is up to you. Having a good relationship with food is way more important than what or how much you eat. If you're a fellow rule-follower who loves guidelines as much as I do, this might be frustrating for you, but *there is no one right way to eat.*

Self-care is not pounding celery juice, tracking every bite, or starving yourself. Those things add stress, which is the opposite of self-care. Nutrition as self-care means eating enough, eating a variety, and eating what makes you feel good, both physically and mentally.

Movement

We were made to move. Movement is a wonderful thing! It lubricates our joints and improves our mood and thinking. It builds strength, stability, and balance. It gives us more energy. It can help alleviate anxiety and depression. It's good for the health of our hearts, our brains, our muscles, and our lungs. Movement just *feels* good and improves our quality of life.

Sadly, culture has distorted movement for a lot of people. For many, exercise has exclusively become a tool for weight loss. Viewing it in this way turns movement into a means to an end, or worse—a punishment. Working out is often done out of fear of gaining weight, which not only contributes to a negative body image, but also sucks the joy out of exercising.

Movement is not any of these things. It is not a means to a certain aesthetic, something you have to do, or a punishment for taking up space. Movement is a loving act of self-love. It is a joyous celebration of life and of your body. It's something you experience because you want to and because it makes your life better. It doesn't have to look a certain way for you to be healthy.

What's the best form of movement? The one you enjoy! As an Enneagram 6, I love to be a part of things, so my preferred ways to move all involve other people. My favorite form of movement is dance. Swing dancing for hours to loud, pulsing jazz music leaves me feeling warm, relaxed, and full of happy brain hormones. I also did crossfit for years because I loved how strong and empowered it made me feel and I also loved the community aspect of it. There's nothing quite like the feeling of getting grimy in an old warehouse with ten other people on a regular basis. Talk about bonding! Long sunset walks with my husband are absolutely delightful. We've recently gotten into the habit of listening to audiobooks on our walks, which means I get to combine several of my absolute favorite things into one activity.

Here's a tip to help you figure out if you really enjoy the form of movement you're doing. Ask yourself this question: would I still be doing this if I knew it would definitely not change my body in any way? If your answer is no, then you probably don't actually enjoy that activity. Consider finding something that you look forward to, not dread. You don't have to be a runner if you hate running with a burning passion. It's never too late to pick up skateboarding or swimming. Oh, and walking certainly *does* count.

Movement doesn't even have to be a formal or structured thing. Movement is vacuuming and tidying up, chasing after your kids, walking to check the mail, or stretching in the morning. Movement is taking regular breaks to go get water when you're working at the office. If you're my husband, movement is shooting a little foam basketball at a hoop strapped to the door a million times a day. We can incorporate joyful movement into our lives without setting aside an hour every day to "exercise."

Clothing

A few months ago I jumped online to buy a new pair of jeans because I noticed that none of mine fit comfortably anymore. Among the reviews, I noticed a handful of women lamenting the fact that they had put on weight during quarantine and that they were just buying "temporary" jeans until they were able to return to their "normal" size.

I bet they were doing better than most. I know there are women out there who refuse to size up to a comfortable fit to punish their bodies for growing. I knew this because I used to be one. I would stubbornly hold on to all my old pants, even ones from high school, determined to fit into them again someday.

Now, I know that I deserve to be able to take full breaths when I'm wearing pants. I know that I don't have to force myself to "pants dance" and smush my way into a size 6 because I'm allowed to change and take up more space. There is zero shame in needing the next size up, or the one after that.

Self-care means buying pants that fit. It means allowing our bodies to change. Let's let go of clothing that no longer fits and treat our bodies with respect. Clothing is supposed to fit us, not the other way around.

Media

Stepping out of places that we've outgrown is not just for

clothing. If you are new to body neutrality, you may find that you're still surrounded by white, thin "fitspo" accounts that promote weight loss. One of the healthiest things you can do for your body image is diversify your media intake.

Diversify your Instagram feed—fill it with body neutral, Anti-Diet accounts. Unfollow accounts that make you feel bad about yourself. Follow bloggers and influencers who look different than you. Follow fat women of color. Read their books, watch their shows, and buy their courses. Celebrate body diversity by filling your life with it. Normalizing normal bodies will make it easier to practice body neutrality.

Rest

We are more stressed out than ever as a culture. Even in 2020, one of the most tumultuous years in recent history, we struggled to slow down. This is because we are bad at resting. We praise productivity. We're married to the grind. We tie our identity to our production. What we neglect to recognize is that who we are is made in the quiet moments. What we can do is determined by how much we rest. If we do not rest, our output will not be sustainable or healthy. We will do what so many modern Westerners before us have done: burn out.

Stress is normal and our bodies know how to handle it. However, our nervous system's stress response is not meant to be activated 24/7. Chronic, never-ending stress is detrimental to our well-being. It wears us down, both physically and mentally.

In a world that celebrates the hustle, rest is a radical form of self-care. Rest can look like many different things. Rest is simply putting down the work and filling your tank back up. It is anything that makes you feel rejuvenated. It can be lighting a candle, reading a book before bed, sitting on the porch with your family, taking a warm bath, sitting outside, or playing music while cooking.

It doesn't have to cost a cent and it doesn't have to take up a lot of time. In fact, it's better if it doesn't. The best form of rest is one you can regularly do. If your only form of rest is a monthly massage or a yearly vacation, you're going to burn out. Ideally, rest is a regular rhythm, woven into your everyday routine. It allows you to build a life you don't need an escape from.

Adequate sleep is another piece of this. Prioritizing your sleep is a simple, but important thing you can do for your body. How do you feel when you wake up early for a workout but feel depleted and exhausted? Do you go back to bed? In moments like those, you have a choice: go through with whatever you have planned despite what you feel, or honor your needs. Although our culture tries to convince you to always do more, maybe what you need is to do *less*. Learn to listen to your body and honor its need for rest.

Because you are enough, you don't need to constantly push yourself to the edge. You can give yourself an abundance of space, restoration, and grace.

CONCLUSION

❖ ❖ ❖

Women have lived long enough under the weight of a societal expectation of beauty. We don't owe anybody beauty. Beauty is not a prerequisite for happiness, success, or womanhood. We are teachers, scientists, nurturers, visionaries, innovators, leaders, entrepreneurs, encouragers, artists, and healers. We are bright, kind, strong, powerful, capable, wise, empowered, and resilient. That is enough. That is more than enough—that is a gift to the world.

In her book *The Beauty Myth*, Naomi Wolf writes, "A culture fixated on female thinness is not an obsession about female beauty, but an obsession about female obedience. Dieting is the most potent political sedative in women's history; a quietly mad population is a tractable one."

We have too much to contribute to the world to be worrying about the approval of anyone who wants to see us subdued by patriarchal cages. Enough with that.

Liberation from negative body image is sacred work. It frees us up to be who we were meant to be. It gives us the freedom to use our gifts fully and unencumbered. It allows us the space to be human, to mess up, to take up space, to try again, to change, and to grow.

You are so much more than a body. Your value is not earned and cannot be taken away from you. You deserve to look at your body with acceptance and respect, knowing that it's the vehicle by which you experience life. No shame. No hiding. No shrinking.

It will not always be easy to practice body neutrality. Many of my favorite old TV shows are filled with fatphobic jokes. It's harder to believe my body is worthy when then characters I love so much are blatantly making fun of fat people. I spent so long priding myself on being a "fit girl" that some of my friends are still confused about why I don't track my calories or my steps anymore. Those conversations are heavy and difficult.

But as hard as it can be at times, it's completely worth it. I can now handle seeing photos of myself that I don't like. The mirror and the scale have no power over my mood anymore. In fact, I haven't even stepped on a scale in months! I don't have to starve myself all day to "save up" for a date night with my husband. I can eat real ice cream with my dad and brothers and not feel like I need to "get back on the bandwagon" on Monday.

Making peace with my body has freed me up to be a more confident, secure version of myself—one who knows she is *loved* and *worthy* no matter what. This simple, scary, radical practice of body neutrality is worth it because it will set you free.

References

Anschutz Health and Wellness Center The CU Anschutz Health and Wellness Center has an entire team devoted to your and your fitness journey! With great content including weekly workouts, & Center, A. (2020, May 07). Just Move: The Six Benefits of Everyday Movement. Retrieved Fall, 2020, from https://anschutzwellness.com/just-move-benefits-everyday-movement/

Bacon, L. (2010). The HAES Manifesto. Retrieved from https://lindobacon.com/HAESbook/pdf_files/HAES_Manifesto.pdf
Bacon, L. (2019, July 08). Fat Is Not the Problem-Fat Stigma Is. Retrieved October 16, 2020, from https://blogs.scientificamerican.com/observations/fat-is-not-the-problem-fat-stigma-is/

Blank, H. (2019, October 15). The Racist Misogyny behind Your "Does My Butt Look Fat in This?": Reading Sabrina Strings' Fearing the Black Body: The Racial Origins of Fat Phobia. Retrieved Fall, 2020, from https://nursingclio.org/2019/10/15/racist-misogyny-behind-your-does-my-butt-look-fat-in-this/

Body Neutrality: A New Way to Relate to Our Bodies. (2017, March 14). Retrieved Fall, 2020, from https://columbuspark.com/2017/03/14/body-neutrality-a-new-way-to-relate-to-our-bodies/

Braveman, P., & Gottlieb, L. (2014). The social determinants of health: it's time to consider the causes of the causes. Public health reports (Washington, D.C. : 1974), 129 Suppl 2(Suppl 2), 19–31. https://doi.org/10.1177/00333549141291S206

Foreman, A. (2015, February 01). Why Footbinding Persisted in China for a Millennium. Retrieved Fall, 2020, from https://www.smithsonianmag.com/history/why-footbinding-persisted-china-millennium-180953971/

Friend, Y. (2019, October 18). The Bizarre and Racist History of the BMI. Retrieved Fall, 2020, from https://elemental.medium.com/the-bizarre-and-racist-history-of-the-bmi-7d8dc2aa33bb

Friend, Y. (2020, July 27). Just Say Fat. Retrieved Fall, 2020, from https://humanparts.medium.com/just-say-fat-c2c28e3bb00

Greenwald, M. (2020, July 21). Unpacking the racist roots of fat phobia and diet culture. Retrieved Fall, 2020, from https://www.intheknow.com/2020/07/13/unpacking-the-racist-roots-of-fat-phobia-and-diet-culture/?guccounter=1

Harrison, C. (2018, August 10). What Is Diet Culture? Retrieved Fall, 2020, from https://christyharrison.com/blog/what-is-diet-culture

Harrison, C. (2018, December 18). Why I'm an Anti-Diet Dietitian-and What That REALLY Means. Retrieved Fall, 2020, from https://christyharrison.com/blog/what-does-anti-diet-really-mean

Kearney-Cooke, A., & Tieger, D. (2015, July 31). Body Image Disturbance and the Development of Eating Disorders. Retrieved October, from https://onlinelibrary.wiley.com/doi/abs/10.1002/9781118574089.ch22

Link Between Social Media & Body Image. (n.d.). Retrieved November 02, 2020, from https://online.king.edu/news/social-media-and-body-image/

Mann, T., Tomiyama, A. J., & Ward, A. (2015). Promoting Public Health in the Context of the "Obesity Epidemic": False Starts and Promising New Directions. Perspectives on psychological science : a journal of the Association for Psychological Science, 10(6), 706–710. https://doi.org/10.1177/1745691615586401

National Eating Disorders Collaboration. (2011). Body Image Fact Sheet. Retrieved from http://www.confidentbody.net/uploads/1/7/0/2/17022536/nedc_body_image_fact_sheet.pdf

Ngo, N. (2019, October 01). What Historical Ideals of Women's Shapes Teach Us About Women's Self-Perception and Body Decisions Today. Retrieved December 02, 2020, from https://journalofethics.ama-assn.org/article/what-historical-ideals-womens-shapes-teach-us-about-womens-self-perception-and-body-decisions-today/2019-10

Oltmann, S. (2014, February 05). N4 Interpersonal relationships and social interaction, FET Colleges, ... Retrieved Fall, 2020, from https://www.slideshare.net/suzaanoltmann/n4-interpersonal-relationships

Perrin, A., & Kumar, M. (2020, May 30). About three-in-ten U.S. adults say they are 'almost constantly' online. Retrieved Fall, 2020, from https://www.pewresearch.org/fact-tank/2019/07/25/americans-going-online-almost-constantly/

Runfola, C. D., Von Holle, A., Trace, S. E., Brownley, K. A., Hofmeier, S. M., Gagne, D. A., & Bulik, C. M. (2013). Body dissatisfaction in women across the lifespan: results of the UNC-SELF and Gender and Body Image (GABI) studies. European eating disorders review : the journal of the Eating Disorders Association, 21(1), 52–59. https://doi.org/10.1002/erv.2201

Siegel, J., Yancey, A., Aneshensel, C., & Schuler, R. (1999, July 16). Body image, perceived pubertal timing, and adolescent mental health. Retrieved Fall, 2020, from https://www.sciencedirect.com/science/article/abs/pii/S1054139X98001608
Statistics & Research on Eating Disorders. (2020, May 08). Retrieved Fall, 2020, from https://www.nationaleatingdisorders.org/statistics-research-eating-disorders

Stice, E., Marti, C. N., Shaw, H., & Jaconis, M. (2009). An 8-year longitudinal study of the natural history of threshold, subthreshold, and partial eating disorders from a community sample of adolescents. Journal of abnormal psychology, 118(3), 587–597. https://doi.org/10.1037/a0016481

Strings, S. (n.d.). The Racist Roots of Fighting Obesity. Retrieved December 02, 2020, from https://www.scientificamerican.com/article/the-racist-roots-of-fighting-obesity2/

Wappler, M. (2019, September 18). Jameela Jamil Isn't Trying to Get Anyone Canceled. Retrieved Fall, 2020, from https://www.glamour.com/story/jameela-jamil-fall-tv-issue

Yeboah, S. (2020, May 29). Why the body positivity movement still has a long way to go. Retrieved Fall, 2020, from https://www.vogue.in/wellness/content/body-positivity-fat-acceptance-movement-still-has-a-long-way-to-go

Printed in Great Britain
by Amazon